English As She Is Wrote: Showing Curious Ways in Which the English Language May Be Made to Convey Ideas Or Obscure Them ; a Companion to "English As She Is Spoke."

Anonymous

Nabu Public Domain Reprints:

You are holding a reproduction of an original work published before 1923 that is in the public domain in the United States of America, and possibly other countries. You may freely copy and distribute this work as no entity (individual or corporate) has a copyright on the body of the work. This book may contain prior copyright references, and library stamps (as most of these works were scanned from library copies). These have been scanned and retained as part of the historical artifact.

This book may have occasional imperfections such as missing or blurred pages, poor pictures, errant marks, etc. that were either part of the original artifact, or were introduced by the scanning process. We believe this work is culturally important, and despite the imperfections, have elected to bring it back into print as part of our continuing commitment to the preservation of printed works worldwide. We appreciate your understanding of the imperfections in the preservation process, and hope you enjoy this valuable book.

No. III.

The Parchment Paper Series.

English
As She is Wrote.

English As She is Wrote,

SHOWING

Curious ways in which the English Language may be made to convey Ideas or obscure them.

A Companion to "English as She is Spoke."

❉❉❉❉

NEW YORK:
D. Appleton & Co., 1, 3, & 5 Bond Street.
[1884.]

15 Sept. 1890.

Mooring Request

COPYRIGHT BY
D. APPLETON AND COMPANY,
1883.

Contents.

		Page
I.	How she is wrote by the Inaccurate	9
II.	By Advertisers and on Sign-boards	20
III.	For Epitaphs	28
IV.	By Correspondents	42
V.	By the Effusive	56
VI.	How she can be oddly wrote	71
VII.	By the Untutored	91

Prefatory.

"ANYBODY," said an astute lawyer, addressing the jury to whom the opposing counsel had reflected upon inaccuracies in the spelling of his brief—"anybody can write English correctly, but surely a man may be allowed to spell a word in two or three different ways if he likes!" This was a claim for independence of action which so commended itself to the jury that it won a verdict for his client.

The same plea may be considered in regard to the truly wonderful way in which the mother-tongue is often written, by the educated sometimes as well as by the uneducated.

A man, it may be urged, has a right to spell as he chooses, and to express his ideas, when he has any, as best he can; while, when he suffers from a dearth of those rare articles, he has still more reason to rejoice in liberty of choice in respect to the language he selects to cover his poverty of thought. Hence there are doubtless good and sufficient reasons for every specimen of "English as she is wrote," which it is the object of this little book to rescue from oblivion, and which have, one and all, been written with the sober conviction, upon the part of the writers, that they accurately conveyed the meaning they desired. Intentionally humorous efforts have been carefully excluded, and the interest of the collection consists in the spontaneity of expression and in the fact that it offers fair samples of the possibilities which lie hidden in the orthography and construction of our language. Let it be remembered, then, that ANYBODY *can write English as she "should be wrote," and hence that a certain meed of admiration is due to those who, exercising their right of independent action, succeed in making it at once origi-*

nal and racy, and in conveying, without the least effort, meanings totally opposed to their intention, affording thereby admirable examples of English as "she is wrote" by thousands.

English as she is wrote.

I.

By the Inaccurate.

In the account of an inaugural ceremony it was asserted that "the procession was very fine, and nearly two miles long, as was also the report of Dr. Perry, the chaplain."

A Western paper says: "A child was run over by a wagon three years old, and cross-eyed, with pantalets on, which never spoke afterward."

Here is some descriptive evidence of personal peculiarities:

"A fellow was arrested with short hair."

"I saw a man digging a well with a Roman nose."

"A house was built by a mason of brown stone."

"Wanted—A room by two gentlemen thirty feet long and twenty feet wide."

"A man from Africa called to pay his compliments tall and dark-complexioned."

"I perceived that it had been scoured with half an eye."

A sea-captain once asserted that his "vessel was beautifully painted with a tall mast."

In an account of travels we are assured that "a pearl was found by a sailor in a shell."

A bill presented to a farmer ran thus: "To hanging two barn doors and myself, 4s. 6d."

A store-keeper assures his customers that "the longest time and easiest terms are given by any other house in the city."

Here is a curious evidence of philanthropy: "A wealthy gentleman will adopt a little boy with a small family."

A parochial report states that "the town farm-house and almshouse have been carried on the past year to our reasonable satisfaction, especially the almshouse, at which there have been an unusual amount of sickness and three deaths."

A Kansas paper thus ends a marriage notice: "The couple left for the East on the night train where they will reside."

In the account of a shipwreck we find the following: "The captain swam ashore. So did the chambermaid; she was insured for a large sum and loaded with pig-iron."

A notice at the entrance to a bridge asserts that "any person driving over this bridge in a faster pace than a walk shall, if a white person be fined five dollars, and if a negro receive twenty-five lashes, half the penalty to be bestowed on the informer."

The following notice appeared on the west end of a country meeting-house: "Anybody sticking bills against this church will be prosecuted according to law or any other nuisance."

A gushing but ungrammatical editor says: "We have received a basket of fine grapes from our friend ——, for which he will please accept our compliments, some of which are nearly one inch in diameter."

On the panel under the letter-receiver of the General Post-Office, Dublin, these words are printed: "Post here letters too late for the next mail."

An Ohio farmer is said to have the following warning posted conspicuously on his premises: "If any man's or woman's cows or oxen gits in this here oats his or her tail will be cut off, as the case may be."

A lady desired to communicate by electricity to her husband in the city the size of an illuminated text which she had promised for the Sunday-school room. When the order reached him it read, "Unto us a child is born, nine feet long by two feet wide."

A farmer who wished to enter some of his live-stock at an agricultural exhibition, in the innocence of his heart, but with more truth in his words than he dreamed of, wrote to the committee, saying, "Enter me for one jackass."

An Irishman complained to his physician that "he stuffed him so much with drugs that he was ill a long time after he got well."

A correspondent of a New York paper described Mr. C.'s journey to Washington to attend "the dying bedside of his mother."

A dealer in engravings announced: "'Scotland Forever.' A Cavalry Charge after Elizabeth Thompson Butler, just published."

A Western paper says that "a fine new school-house has just been finished in that town capable of accommodating three hundred students four stories high."

A coroner's verdict read thus: "The deceased came to his death by excessive drinking, producing apoplexy in the minds of the jury."

An old edition of Morse's geography declares that "Albany has four hundred dwelling-houses and twenty-four hundred inhabitants, all standing with their gable-ends to the street."

A member of a school committee writes, "We have two school-rooms sufficiently large to accommodate three hundred pupils, one above the other."

A Harrisburg paper, answering a correspondent on a question of etiquette, says: "When a gentleman and lady are walking upon the street, the lady should walk inside of the gentleman."

A clergyman writes, "A young woman died in my neighborhood yesterday, while I was preaching the gospel in a beastly state of intoxication."

A certain friendly society, which was also a sort of mutual insurance organization, had this among its printed notices to the members: "In the event of your death, you are requested to bring your book, policy, and certificate at once to Mr. ——, when your claims will have immediate attention."

A New York paper, describing a funeral in Jersey City, says: "At the ferry four friends of the deceased took possession of the carriage and followed the remains to Evergreen Cemetery, where they were quietly interred in a new lot without service or ceremony." The devotion of the friends of the deceased was certainly remarkable, but one can not help wondering what became of the remains.

A newspaper gives an account of a man who "was driving an old ox when he became angry and kicked him, hitting his jawbone with such force as to break his leg." "We have been fairly wild ever since we read the paper," writes a contemporary, "to know who or which got angry at whom or what, and if the ox kicked the man's jaw with such force as to break the ox's leg, or how it is. Or did the man kick the ox in the jawbone with such force as to break the ox's leg, and, if so, which leg? It's one of those things which no man can find out, save only the man who kicked or was being kicked, as the case may be."

One of Sir Boyle Roche's invitations to an Irish nobleman was rather equivocal. He wrote, "I hope, my lord, if you ever come within a mile of my house you will stay there all night."

A German tourist expresses himself in regard to his Scottish experiences as follows: "A person angry says to-day that he was from the theatre gallary spit upon. Very fine. I also was spit upon. Not on the dress but into the eye strait it came with strong force while I look up angry to the gallary. Befor I come to your country I worship the Scotland of my books, my 'Waverly Novel,' you know, but now I dwell here since six months, in all parts, the picture change. I now know of the bad smell, the oath and curse of God's name, the wisky drink and the rudeness. You have much money here, but you want what money can not buye—heart cultivating that makes respect for gentle things. O! to be spit in the eye in one half million of peopled town. Let me no longer be in this cold country, where people push in the street, blow the noze with naked finger, empty the dish at the house door, chooze the clergy from the lower classes and then go with them to death for an ecclesiastical theory which none of them can understand. I go home three days time." There is more in this than grotesque English, however. It abounds with good sense and penetration.

The following is a pattern piece of modern style, sanctioned by an English Board of Trade, and drawn up by an eminent authority: "Tickets are nipped at the Barriers, and passengers admitted to the platforms will have to be delivered up to the Company in event of the holders subsequently retiring from the platforms without travelling, and cannot be recognized for readmission."

A college professor, describing the effect of the wind in some Western forests, wrote, "In traveling along the road, I even sometimes found the logs bound and twisted together to such an extent that a mule couldn't climb over them, so I went round."

A mayor in a university town issued the following proclamation: " Whereas a Multiplicity of Dangers are often incurred by Damage of outrageous Accidents by Fire, we whose names are undesigned have thought proper that the Benefit of an Engine bought by us for the better extinguishing of which by the Accidents of Almighty God may unto us happen to make a Rate togather Benevolence for the better propagating such useful Instruments."

II.

By Advertisers and on Sign-boards.

Two young women want washing.

Teeth extracted with great pains.

Babies taken and finished in ten minutes by a country photographer.

Wood and coal split.

Wanted, a female who has a knowledge of fitting boots of a good moral character.

For sale, a handsome piano, the property of a young lady who is leaving Scotland in a walnut case with turned legs.

A large Spanish blue gentleman's cloak lost in the neighborhood of the market.

To be sold, a splendid gray horse, calculated for a charger, or would carry a lady with a switch tail.

Wanted, a young man to take charge of horses of a religious turn of mind.

A lady advertises her desire for a husband "with a Roman nose having strong religious tendencies."

Wanted, a young man to look after a horse of the Methodist persuasion.

A chemist inquires, "Will the gentleman who left his stomach for analysis please call and get it, together with the result?"

Wanted, an accomplished poodle nurse. Wages, $5.00 a week.

In the far West a man advertises for a woman "to wash, iron and milk one or two cows."

Lost a cameo brooch representing Venus and Adonis on the Drumcondra Road about 10 o'clock on Tuesday evening.

An advertiser, having made an advantageous purchase, offers for sale, on very low terms, "six dozen of prime port wine, late the property of a gentleman forty years of age, full of body, and with a high bouquet."

A steamboat-captain, in advertising for an excursion, closes thus: "Tickets, 25 cents; children half price, to be had at the captain's office."

Among carriages to be disposed of, mention is made of "a mail phaeton, the property of a gentleman with a moveable head as good as new."

An inducement to return property is offered as follows: "If the gentleman who keeps the shoe store with a red head will return the umbrella of a young lady with whalebone ribs and an iron handle to the slate-roofed grocer's shop, he will hear of something to his advantage, as the same is a gift of a deceased mother now no more with the name engraved upon it."

An English matrimonial advertisement reads as follows: "A young man about 25 years of Age, in a very good trade, whose Father will make him worth £1000, would willingly embrace a suitable MATCH. He has been brought up a Dissenter with his Parents, and is a sober man."

A landlady, innocent of grammatical knowledge, advertises that she has "a fine, airy, well-furnished bedroom for a gentleman twelve feet square"; another has "a cheap and desirable suit of rooms for a respectable family in good repair"; still another has "a hall bedroom for a single woman 8 × 12."

A photographer's sign reads: "This style 3 pictures finished in fifteen minutes while you wait for twenty-five cents beautifully colored."

A cheap restaurant displays this sign: "Oyster pies open all night," and "Coffee and cakes off the griddle."

A baker displays the sign, "Family Baking Done Here." The sign would look more appropriate if it were in front of some of our "cool and well-ventilated" summer-resort hotels.

The sign at Abraham Lowe's inn, Douglas, Isle of Man, is accompanied by this quaint verse:

"I'm Abraham Lowe, and half way up the hill,
If I were higher up wat's funnier still,
I should be Lowe. Come in and take your fill
Of porter, ale, wine, spirits what you will.
Step in, my friend, I pray no further go,
My prices, like myself, are always low."

On a vacant lot back of Covington, Kentucky, is posted this sign: "No plane base Boll on these Primaces."

Notice in a Hoboken ferry-boat: "The seats in this cabin are reserved for ladies. Gentlemen are requested not to occupy them until the ladies are seated."

A sign in a Pennsylvania town reads as follows: "John Smith, teacher of cowtillions and other dances—grammar taut in the neatest manner—fresh salt herrin on draft—likewise Goodfreys cordjial—rutes sassage and other garden truck—N. B. bawl on friday nite—prayer meetin chuesday—also salme singing by the quire."

The following notice appeared on the fence of a vacant lot in Brooklyn: "All persons are forbidden to throw ashes on this lot under penalty of the law or any other garbage."

A barber's sign in Buffalo, N. Y., has the following: "This is the place for physiognomical hair-cutting and ecstatic shaving and shampooing."

A San Francisco boot-black, of poetic aspirations, proclaims his superior skill in the following lines, pasted over the door of his establishment:

"No day was e'er so bright,
So black was never a night,
As will your boots be, if you get
Them blacked right in here, you bet!"

The following appears on a Welsh shoemaker's sign-board: "Pryce Dyas Coblar, dealer in Bacco Shag and Pig Tail Bacon and Ginarbread, Eggs laid by me, and very good Paradise in the summer, Gentlemen and Lady can have good Tae and Crumpets and Straw berry with a scim milk, because I can't get no cream. N. B. Shuse and Boots mended very well."

An Irish inn exhibits the following in large type:

"Within this hive we're all alive,
　　With whiskey sweet as honey;
If you are dry, step in and try,
　　But don't forget your money."

An inn near London displays a board with the following inscription:

"*Call*—Softly,
　Drink Moderately,
　Pay *Honourably*,
　Be good Company,
　Part FRIENDLY,
　Go HOME quietly.
Let those lines be no MAN'S sorrow,
Pay to DAY and i'll TRUST tomorrow."

III.

For Epitaphs.

A TERSE account of an untimely end is given upon a stone in a Mexican church-yard:

"He was young, he was fair
But the Injuns raised his hair."

The following may be read upon the tombstone of Lottie Merrill, the young huntress of Wayne County, Pennsylvania: "Lottie Merrill lays hear she dident know wot it wuz to be afeered but she has hed her last tussel with the bars and theyve scooped her she was a good girl and she is now in heaven. It took six big bars to get away with her. She was only 18 years old."

Upon the tomb of a boy who died of eating too much fruit, this quaint epitaph conveys a moral:

"*Currants* have check'd the *current* of my blood,
  And *berries* brought me to be *buried* here;
Pears have *par'd* off my body's hardihood,
  And *plums* and *plumbers spare* not one so *spare*.
Fain would I *feign* my fall; so *fair* a *fare*
Lessens not hate, yet 'tis a *lesson* good.
Gilt will not long hide *guilt*, such thin washed *ware*
Wears quickly, and its *rude* touch soon is *rued*.
Grave on my *grave* some sentence *grave* and terse,
That *lies* not as it *lies* upon my clay,
But in a gentle *strain* of *unstrained* verse,
Prays all to pity a poor patty's *prey*,
Rehearses I was fruitful to my *hearse*,
Tells that my days are *told*, and soon I'm *toll'd* away."

In Glasgow Cathedral is an epitaph, which is engraved on the lid of a very old sarcophagus, discovered in the crypt:

"Our Life's a flying Shadow, God's the Pole,
The Index pointing at him is our Soul,
Death's the Horizon, when our Sun is set,
Which will through Chryst a Resurrection get."

In a grave-yard at Montrose, in Scotland, this inscription may still be seen:

"Here lies the Body of
George Young
And of all his posterity for
fifty years backwards."

This brief announcement may be read in Wrexham church-yard, Wales:

"Here lies five babies and children dear
Three at Owestry and two here."

In a church-yard near London the following may be deciphered:

"Killed by an omnibus why not?
So quick a death a boon is
Let not his friends lament his lot
For mors omnibus communis."

There is an unqualified Hibernianism in the following:

"Here lies the remains of
Thomas Melstrom who died
in Philadelphia March 17th
Had he lived he would have
been buried here."

A good deal of positive information is conveyed in this epitaph:

"Here lies, cut down like unripe fruit
The wife of Deacon Amos Shute;
She died of drinking too much coffee,
Anny dominy eighteen forty."

To the victim of an accident:

"Here lies the body of James Hambrick which was accidentally shot in the Pacas River by a young man with one of Colts large revolvers with no stopper for the hand for to rest on. It was one of the old fashioned sort, brass mounted and of such is the Kingdom of Heaven."

William Curtis, who was famous for his bad grammar, may have composed his own epitaph:

" Here lies William Curtis
Our late Lord Mayor
Who has left this world,
And gone to that there."

In a church-yard in London, evidently written by a Cockney:

"Here lies John Ross.
Kicked by a Hoss."

In Trinity church-yard, New York, this inscription may be read:

"Val. ——
　　　Sidney Breese.
　　　June 9 17—.
　　　Made by himself.
　　Ha! Sidney, Sidney
　　　Liest thou here?
　　　　I lye here
　Till Times last Extremity."

Upon a stone, under the Grocers' Arms, is this inscription, in memory of Garrard, a tea-dealer:

"Garret some called him
　　But that was too lye
　His name is Garrard
　　Who now here doth lye
　Weepe not for him
　　Since he is gone before
　To heaven where Grocers
　　There are many more."

The value of phonetic spelling is set forth in this terse memorial:

"Here lies two brothers by misfortune surrounded
One died of his wounds, the other was drounded."

Resignation and an eye to the main chance are combined in the following:

"Beneath this stone, in hope of Zion
Doth lie the landlord of the Lion,
His son keeps in the business still
Resigned unto the heavenly Will."

In a church-yard in Wiltshire, England:

"Beneath this stone lies our dear child
Whos' gone away from we
For evermore into eternity;
When we do hope that we shall go to he
But him can never come back to we."

On Mrs. Sarah Newman:

"Pain was my portion
    Physic was my food
Groans was my devotion
    Drugs done me no good.
Christ was my physician
    Knew what way was best
To ease me of my pain
    He took my soul to rest."

An inscription to four wives:

"To the memory of my four wives, who all died within the space of ten years, but more perteckler to the last Mrs. Sally Horne who has left me and four dear children, she was a good, *sober* and *clean* soul and may i soon go to her.

"Dear wives if you and i shall all go to heaven,
    The Lord be blest for then we shall be even.

      "William Joy Horne, Carpenter."

On a dyer:

"He died to live and lived to dye."

On Mrs. Lee and her son:

"In her life she did her best
Now I hope her soul's at rest.
Also her son Tom lies at her feet
He lived till he made both ends meet."

At Edinburgh:

"John Mc pherson
Was a wonderful person
He stood 6 ft 2 without his shoe
And he was slew.
At Waterloo."

One John Round was lost at sea, and in the grave-yard of his native place a stone was erected with the following couplet inscribed thereon:

"Under this bed lies John Round
Who was lost at sea and never found."

In an old church-yard in Ireland:

"Here lies John Highley whose father and mother were drownded on their passage to America. Had they lived they would have been buried here."

In a church-yard in Ohio:

"Under this sod
    And under these trees
Lieth the Bod
    Y of Solomon Pease.
He's not in this hole
    But only his pod.
He shelled out his soul
    And went up to his God."

From a tombstone in Cornwall, England:

"Father and mother and I
  Lie buried here asunder;
Father and mother lie buried here,
  And I lie buried yonder."

On Eliza Newman:

"Like a tender Rose Tree was my Spouse to me;
Her offspring Pluckt too long deprived of life was she.
Three went before. Her Life went with the Six
I stay with 3 Our sorrows for to mix
Till Christ our only hope, Our Joys doth fix."

On a drummer, in an English church-yard:

"Tom Clark was a drummer, who went to the war,
And was killed by a bullet, and his soul sent for;
There were no friends to mourn him, for his virtues were rare,
He died like a man, and like a Christian bear."

On a stone near Appomattox Court-house, Virginia:

"Robert C Wright was born June 26th 1772 Died July 2. 1815 by the blood thrusty hand of John Sweeny Sr Who was massacred with the Nife then a London Gun discharge a ball penetrate the Heart that give the immortal wound."

At Middletown, Connecticut, is the following:

"This lovely, pleasant child—
  He was our only one,
Altho' we've buried three before—
  Two daughters and a son."

The controlling power of rhyme is well illustrated in the subjoined, from a tombstone in Manchester:

"Here lies alas! more's the pity,
  All that remains of Nicholas Newcity.
     "N. B.—His name was Newtown."

Another instance of how rhyming difficulties may be overcome is as follows:

"Here lies the remains of Thomas Woodhen,
  The most amiable of husbands and excellent of men.

"N. B.—His real name was Woodcock, but it wouldn't come in rhyme. *His Widow.*"

The subjoined contains a solemn warning:

"My wife has left me, she's gone up on high,
  She was thoughtful while dying, and said 'Tom, don't cry.'
She was a great beauty, so every one knows,
With Hebe like features and a fine Roman nose;
She played the piany, and was learning a ballad,
When she sickened and die-did from eating veal salad."

Upon a tombstone in Pennsylvania:

"Battle of Shiloh.
April 6 1862
John D L was born March 26 1839 in the town of West Dresden State of New York where the wicked cease from troubling and the weary are at rest."

A tombstone in Pittsfield, Massachusetts, has these lines:

"When you my friends are passing by,
And this inform you where I lie,
Remember you ere long must have,
Like me, a mansion in the grave,
Also 3 infants, 2 sons and a daughter."

IV.

By Correspondents.

From a butcher at Berhampoor, India, to a customer:

"To his Highness—Kid Esquire

"The humble butcher, Nows Rouny, Restpectfully sheweth that for your honor has sent a good beef, 1 rump and pleased to take it and pay day labor of bearer coolly. As your obedient butcher shall ever pray."

From a scholar in India to his master:

"My dear Sir: I humbly beg to inform you pleas to give me leaf for one week because I cannot walk with my feet, I am very uncomfortable. Give my compliments to My Master. I pray to God for Everlasting life. I am your humble Servant   Shebart Lall."

From an Indian school-boy:
"Benevolent Sir: The wolf of sickness has laid hold on the flock of my health."

From an Indian clerk:
"Sir. Being afflicted to the stomach and vomiteng I am sorry I cannot attend to office today."

From a Canadian lady to eligible gentleman:
"Dear Mr. B. I, Mrs. Wigston wish you would call on my daughter Amelia. She is very amusing and is a regular young flirt. She can sing like a hunny bee and her papa can play on the fiddle nicely and we might have a rare ho-down. Amelia is highely educated, she can dance like a grasshoper looking for grub and she can meke beautiful bread, it tastes just

like hunny bees' bread and for pumpkin pies she can't be beat. In fact she's ahead of all F girls and will make a good wife for any man.

"Yours truly

"Mrs. Wigston.

"Bring your brother."

From a school-boy to the elder Booth:

"West House School. Prospect N. Y.
"Dear Sur and Frend.

"Heering that you was going to come to Uttica to perform in a play called Hamlit I would like to say that us boys is gitting up a Exibition for the benefit of diseased soldiers and their widows and orfans and would like to engage you to do the leading part. I have talked it up with the boys and we will do the squire thing by you and I am arterised to make you the following offer. We will come doun after you with a good conveyance and will give you at the rate of 10 dollars a day and

board and shall want you one week. If you think it necessary you can have one or two of our best women actors to come up with you but we can't pay them over three dollars a day and feed. You can have some fun at a hunting deer and foxes around Flamburgs and Ed Wilkisun's. Pleas let me know as soon as you can.
"Yours truly James Sweet.
"If you come callating to hunt get Frank Meyer's hound she is a good one."

We subjoin several letters received by a New York publishing house:

"—— La, Nov 18, 188–.
"Dear Sir. I have seated my self down to pen you a few lines in reguards off your high degrode Tex Books Sir I wish you would forward to me in the next Mail a Cataloudge off all of your Edgucational old and latest publish books in Market I stand in need off a good set of books and when I receive your Cataloudge

I will send on immeadily and get a Selecticed outfit of your books. By so doing you will oblidge yours & Etc."

"dear Sr I saw A smawl list of yours embraces standard works in every department of study and for every grade of classes from the *primary* school to the *university* I desire to have correspondence with you and as I taught school for threw 3 seson in the ninth district of Fuentress County tennessee and i quit eimet with Cooper and our country need instruction and except we get the implement for instruction we may all ways espect ignorant. turn over. Mr I want you to send educational list of your standard works and also A copy Book that I may instruct my studentes more correctly and I profer to take Agents if hit is not contrary to law if your work can sold with out paing tax or lison

"and A blige youres truley Joel E Atkinson school teacher 9 deistrict Fuentress co Logan Finch Chareles Atkinson J Hall e school directers in my distreetes."

"Dear Sir I want you to send me a catalogue the Emblem book and tell me what it will cost I think I can Sell as Many as Fifteen be sure and give the Price that is what they want to know Dear Sir I Received your Copy Oct 9th 1881 if you charge Any thing for composeing them letters write to me and I will pay will Send it by Mail in one cent stamps you need not to think I want to swinle you out of one cent I will do Every thing I say I will do So if you will write and give the Price of the Emblem and the love writer and chart and key of the Spenserion cystem and they like I will get up a subscription and send the Money for them immediately Dear Sir tell me what is the Emblem of a red rose and white rose of a boca."

"Dear Sir:

"Wilt please send me a description of your outfit of Books and give me one or two iedies abought the catalogue price of your English, Latin Greek brench and stanish Italian Hebrew and Siyuriak books to my address. I has issued out orders bot comisition &c—my trustee tell me that only two D V z and in New York at the time it Feby. the 15 my No of books is twenty five and I desire one complet Example of your best books if you can Conven-'y furnish my needs wright at once I will be more an obliged to you. Looking by every mail for your returns Soon, so please your truly servant

  "I am dear Sir:
   "My name in Full
    "✱ ✱ ✱ ✱."

"Dear Sir:

"Understanding that You possess some Influnce among the Bord of Directors of your fine books and for useful learning for Schools I beg to Solicit your interest for Me I want to Purchase Some Usful Books and Messrs please send me one of your Cataloges you well obligde me Much in so doing. & Far my Friends I Will tell You I have a great many of Relitives who would wish to Purchase some book if could be bought from you below Price My Frend you must excuse my Hasty note for the Small time Was at Hand and all so my Frend you must excuse my Led Pensel. Wright my soon Frend I will close and will shew you that you will be remembered by Sirs Your Obedient & Fathful Servants ——."

"Sir: I now write to you to ask you information on book lines Sir. i have seen some of your books and the suited me very much on Edjucational and Sir i did suspect to start To Teach School in the Same Ward And i Wanted to get a fenel Resortment of of Books and i

Wanted To get My books from you and i
Wanted Like to know how you Would Reply
me them And i hope when you Riseived this
Letter that you Would Write Wright away
At once And give me the full Address how to
send for These Books And i Want to Know
Wethe I give you the Wright Address Sir
your Friend —— Would like To Read A Letter from under your Hand And i Want you
To please To give me your Address of All
kines of Books that yu have i Exspect to start
School soon & i had much Applications By
pupils that Lives A. Rounds in the Sections
Where i Lives ses ef i gets the Books they
Would Buy them from me i hope that you
Would Wright As Soon as Posable And Let
me know so that i Can Write Again And please
To Send me some of your paper so that i Can
Read them to the people so Them Can Believe
that i did wrote here When you Write please
To Direct your Letter to —— so i hope you

Will Write Soon And please fail not To Send me some of your Papers And Direct me how To Get Money to you When i Send for Books fail not To Direct your Letter to —— Post-office. So i have no more to Write i Will Close & Remain "Your Truly Friend."

"M—— Ala.
"Oct 13th 1881. Dear Sir Dear Friend you will please Send me one line of capitals letters one line of the small letters and Show me the space how far up and how far down and write & tell me what the chart and frey with cost, the chart of the Standard System is the one I want. there is Eight men I have shewn your copy you sent to me they say they intend to have one chart a piece Dear Sir I have been talking with Several young Men about love writers I want you to compose three letters consisting of love and poetry write one as though you loved her and want

to marry her. one as though she had Slighted you. the Next one as you think best Compose them and Send them to me and I will shew them to the Boys I am satisfied they will be sure to by."

Letter to an editor:

"Dear Sir—:

"The hystoric apple that tossed about and struck Sir Isaac Newton landed finally, in revealing its inner nature its hidden meaning, not only as a consolation but also of universal utility in all scientific branges:

"Or out of the simbols of the ancient World, up to the real discoveries of the present time proceeded the solution of the relation of the Eternal time, motion, and distance. Which set forte the discovery of the generational cosmological Parents of this planet, are discovered that these can be seen by all mankind.

"Resp."

By Correspondents.

Letter received by a cotton-broker:

"Flat Town Dec. 30th

"Messrs.

"J—— W—— & Co

"Sir. Gentlemen.

"The shipments from this out the balance of the season will be for more on the count. last year was a short crop and two weeks erly than this season and people sold rite strate a long here last season and the biggest and best farmers this season are holding looking forward to Biger prices I have gathered 80 bales and 15 or 16 more in the field yet to pick so you see when I make my estimate in this county they are a power of cotton on the fields yet to pick and a grate eel in houses not gined up yet, gust act as if those deals were your own shood you close them out gust credit my account with the profitts but dont close them out until you think it has tuch bottom then I want you to by me the same amount but don't by till you think it the rite time and then shood you see a proffit in it Turn it loose without ever consulting me if it clears up cold we will have Kilan frost but it can't hurt here for the crop is made.

"I remain yours very truly."

Another letter to a cotton-broker:

"Messrs. W—— W—— & Co.
"Sir Gents

"I have gust got in form the West and find your letter stating that corn had touched bottom which I do think myself it has, but it has avanced so much now I don't noe that it wood pay me much either way now. had I bin at home I shood of closed out and of Bout the same amount was my Idee. we are from ten days to fully two weeks backwards with our crops owing to our wet weather but that donte say they won't be as much made as was last year while we are backward there are more fertilizers yoused than ware last year and more Acreage our country is in a better condision to make a crop and I expect the west ginerally that way at the same time I am only one neighbourhood. pleas let me hear from you more fully on the matter hoping to hear from you soon I remain

"yours verry truly
"I will act according to your council."

A Georgia merchant received a short time since the following order from a customer: "Mr. B——, please send me $1 worth of coffy and $1 worth of shoogar, some small nales. My wife had a baby last nite, also two padlocks and a monkey rench."

V.

By the Effusive.

PROFESSOR HUXLEY is credited with the assertion that the primrose is "a corollifloral dicotyledonous exogen, with a monopetalous corolla and a central placenta."

A reporter with a large imagination, writing about the decoration of a church at a fashionable wedding in this city, said that "the church was ensconced in flowers."

A scientific writer defines sneezing as "a phenomenon provoked either by an excitation brought to bear on the nasal membrane or by a sudden shock of the sun's rays on the membranes of the eye. This peripheral irritation is transmitted by the trifacial nerve to the Gasserian ganglion, whence it passes by a commissure to an agglomeration of globules in the medulla oblongata or in the protuberance; from this point, by a series of numerous reflex and complicated acts, it is transformed by the mediation of the spinal cord into a centrifugal excitation which radiates outward by means of the spinal nerves to the expiratory muscles."

The school committee in Massachusetts recommend exercises in English composition in these terms:

"Next to the pleasure that pervades the corridors of the soul when it is entranced by the whiling witchery that presides over it consequent upon the almost divine productions of Mozart, Haydn, and Handel, whether these are executed by magician concert parts in deep and highly matured melody from artistic modulated intonations of the finely cultured human voice, or played by some fairy-fingered musician upon the trembling strings of the harp or piano, comes the charming delight we experience from the mastery of English prose, and the spell-binding wizards of song who by their art of divination through their magic wand, the pen, have transformed scenes hitherto unknown and made them as immortal as those spots of the Orient and mountain haunts of the gods, whether of sunny Italy or of tuneful, heroic Greece."

A farmer's daughter expresses herself in the following terms:

"Dear Miss:

"The energy of the race prompts me to assure you that my request is forbidden, the idea of which I awkwardly nourished, notwithstanding my propensity to reserve. Mr. T will be there—Let me with confidence assure you that him and brothers will be very happy to meet you and brothers. Us girls cannot go, for reasons. The attention of cows claims our assistance this evening.

"Unalterably yours."

The following is probably the longest sentence ever written, containing, as it does, eight hundred words:

"I propose, then, to give your readers some description of this old yet still strange and wild country, that has been settled for three hundred years, and is not yet inhabited—a land of shifting sand and deep mud—a land of noble rivers that rise in swamps and consist merely of chains of shallow lakes, some of them twenty miles long and two miles across, and only twelve feet deep—of wide, sandy plains, covered with solemn-sounding pines—of spots so barren that nothing can be made to grow upon them, and yet with a soil so fertile that if you tickle it with a hoe, it will laugh out an abundant harvest of sugar, cotton, and fruit — a land of oranges, lemons, pomegranates, pineapples, figs, and bananas; whose rivers teem with fish, its forests with game, and its very air with fowl; where everything will grow except apples and wheat; where everything can be found except ice; yet where the people, with a productive soil, a mild climate and beautiful nature, affording every table luxury, live on corn-grist, sweet potatoes, and molasses; where men possessing forty thousand head of cattle never saw a glass of milk in their lives, using the imported article when used at all, and then calling it consecrated milk; where the very effort to milk a cow would probably scare her to death, as well as frighten a whole neighborhood by the unheard of phenomenon; where cabbages grow on the tops of trees, and you may dig bread out of the ground; where, below the frost-line, the castor-oil plant becomes a large tree of several years' growth, and a pumpkin or bean-vine will take root from its trailing branches, and thus spread and live year after year; where cattle do not know what hay is, and refuse it when offered, so that the purchase of a yoke of oxen is not considered valid if the animals will not eat in a stable; and where in the mild winter, when the land grass is dried up, horses and cattle may be seen wading and swimming in the ponds and streams, plunging their heads under water grasses and moss; where many lakes have holes in the bottom and underground communication, so that they will sometimes shrink away to a mere cupful, leaving many square miles of surface uncovered, and then again fill up from below and spread out over their former area; where some of them have outlets in the ocean far from shore, bursting up a perpetual spring of fresh water in the very midst of the briny saltness of the sea;

where in times of low water, during a long exhaustive dry season, men have gone under ground in one of these subterranean rivers, from lake to lake, a distance of eight miles; where the ground will sometimes sink and the cavity fill with water, until tall trees, that had stood and sunk upright, will have their topmost branches deeply covered; where rivers will disappear in the earth and rise again, thus forming natural bridges, some of them a mile in breadth; where, instead of spring, summer, autumn, and winter, there are two seasons only —eight months summer, and four months warm weather; where the winter is the dry season, and the summer almost a daily rain; where, in order to take a walk, you first wade through a light sand ankle deep and then get into a mud-puddle, and some of these mud-puddles cover a whole county; where no clay is found fit for brick-making, and people build houses without chimneys; where to make a living is so easy a task, that every one possesses the laziness of ten ordinary men, every one you wish to employ in labor says he is tired and would seem to have been born so; where ague would prevail if the people would take the trouble to shake; where a large orange-tree will bear several thousand oranges—leaves, buds, blossom, half-grown and full-grown fruit, all at once—and every twenty-five feet square of sand will sustain such a tree; where, in many parts, cold weather is an impossibility, and perpetual verdure reigns; where the Everglades are found, covering many large counties with water from one to six feet deep, with a bottom, mud covered, yet underneath solid and firm, from which grasses grow up to the surface—a sea of green, and with islands large and small scattered over the surface, covered with live oaks and dense vegetation; where alligators, or gators as they are called in Florida parlance, possess undoubted aboriginal rights of citizenship, and mosquitoes pay constant visits and are instructive and even penetrating in their attention to strangers."

An Irish paper contained this account of Mrs. Siddons's appearance:

"On Sunday, Mrs. Siddons, about whom all the world has been talking, exposed her beautiful, adamantine, soft, and lovely person, for the first time at Smock Alley Theatre in the bewitching, melting, and all tearful character of Isabella. From the repeated panegyrics of the impartial London newspapers, we were taught to expect the sight of a heavenly angel, but how were we supernaturally surprised into almost awful joy at beholding a mortal goddess! The house was crowded with hundreds more than it could hold, with thousands of admiring spectators who went away without a sight. This extraordinary phenomenon of tragic excellence! this star of Melpomene! this comet of the stage! this sun of the firmament of the Muses! this moon of blank verse! this queen and princess of tears! this Donellan of the poisoned dagger! this empress of pistol and dagger! this chaos of Shakespeare! this world of weeping clouds! this Juno commanding aspects! this Terpsichore of the curtains and scenes! this Proserpine of fire and excitement! this Katterfelto of wonders! exceeded expectation, went beyond belief and soared above all the natural powers of description! She was nature itself! She was the most exquisite work of art! She was the very daisy, primrose, tuberose, sweet brier, furze blossom, gilliflower, wall flower, cauliflower, auricula, and rosemary! In short, she was the bouquet of Parnassus! When expectations were so high, it was thought she would be injured by her appearance, but it was the audience who were injured: several fainted before the curtain drew up! When she came to the scene of parting with her wedding ring, ah! what a sight was there! the very fiddlers in the orchestra, albeit unused to melting mood, blubbered like hungry children crying for their bread and butter! and when the bell rang for music between the acts the tears ran from the bassoon players' eyes in such plentiful showers that they choked the finger stops, and making a spout of the instrument poured in such torrents on the first fiddler's book that not seeing the overture was in two sharps, the leader of the band played it in one flat. But the sobs and sighs of the groaning audience and the noise of corks drawn from smelling bottles prevented the mistakes between sharps and flats being heard. One hundred and nine ladies fainted! forty-six went into fits! and ninety-five had strong hysterics. The world will scarcely credit the truth when they are told that fourteen children, five old men, one hundred tailors, and six common councilmen were actually drowned in the inundation of tears that flowed from the galleries, the slips, and the boxes, to increase the briny pond in the pit. The water was three feet deep. An Act of Parliament will certainly be passed against her playing any more!"

Few poems have been more generally admired or paraphrased in the various tongues of earth than that commencing with the lines—

> "Mary had a little lamb,
>   Its fleece was white as snow,
>   And everywhere that Mary went
>   This lamb was sure to go."

The story is current at the national capital that Mr. Evarts, when Secretary of State, on one occasion, in a jocular crowd of his friends, was desired to condense into prose these immortal verses. Urgently solicited, Mr. Evarts yielded, and wrote as follows:

"Mary, a female, judged to be of the race of man, whose family name is unknown, whether of native or foreign birth, of lofty or lowly lineage, and whose appearance, manners, and mental cultivation are involved in the most profound mystery, which probably will never be fully ascertained unless through the most profound researches of an historian admirably trained in his profession, who shall devote the ablest efforts of his life to the investigation of the subject, uninfluenced by either passion or prejudice, and having only in view the sacred truth, at the same time being utterly regardless of the plaudits or censures of the world, we are informed by one who, it has been stated, at one time while living in that part of the United States of America known as Massachusetts, whose fishermen have frequently been involved in difficulties with the authorities of her Majesty Queen Victoria, Queen of Great Britain and Empress of the Indies, whose domains extended over a large share of the habitable globe, thereby endangering the peace which should so happily exist between nations of the same blood and language, had an infant sheep, of which there are many millions of various stocks and qualities now in our country, constantly adding wealth and prosperity to our republic, and enabling us to be entirely independent of all other nations for our supply of wool, now ample for the use of factories already busily employed, and for those which ere long will be constructed in all parts of our land, working both by water and steam power, and in whatever direction the said Mary traveled, this animal, whose fleece was snow-white, even as the lofty mountain-regions in the silent solitudes of eternal winter, as the ethereal vapors which oft float over an autumnal sky, 'darkly, deeply, beautifully blue,' or as the lacteal fluid covered with masses of delicate froth, found in the buckets of the rosy dairymaid, whether meandering through the meadows in midsummer, gathering the luscious strawberry, strolling in the woodland paths in search of wild flowers, visiting the church with her uncles, cousins, and aunts, to listen to the inspired words which come from the lips of the minister of the sanctuary, or when retiring to her blissful couch to seek rest and enjoy sweet repose after the cares and labors of the day; in fact, 'everywhere that Mary went' this youthful sheep, influenced doubtless by that affection which is oft so conspicuously manifested by the lower animals in their association with human beings, was ever observed to accompany her."

VI.

How she can be Oddly Wrote.

THE following amusing rhyme clipped from an old paper shows to advantage some of the peculiarities of the English language:

SALLY SALTER.

Sally Salter, she was a young teacher, that taught,
And her friend Charley Church was a preacher, who praught;
Though his friends all declared him a screecher, who scraught.

His heart, when he saw her, kept sinking, and sunk,

And his eyes, meeting hers, kept winking, and wunk;
While she, in her turn, fell to thinking, and thunk.

He hastened to woo her, and sweetly he wooed,
For his love for her grew—to a mountain it grewed,
And what he was longing to do, then he doed.

In secret he wanted to speak, and he spoke:
To seek with his lips what his heart had long soke;
So he managed to let the truth leak, and it loke.

He asked her to ride to the church and they rode;
They so sweetly did glide, that they both thought they glode,
And they came to the place to be tied, and were tode.

Then "Homeward," he said, "let us drive,"
    and they drove,
As soon as they wished to arrive they arrove;
For whatever he couldn't contrive she con-
    trove.

The kiss he was dying to steal, then he stole,
At the feet where he wanted to kneel, there he
    knole,
And he said, "I feel better than ever I fole."

So they to each other kept clinging, and clung,
While Time his swift circuit was winging, and
    wung;
And this was the thing he was bringing, and
    brung:

The man Sally wanted to catch, and had caught—
That she wanted from others to snatch, and
    had snaught,
Was the one that she now liked to scratch, and
    she scraught.

And Charley's warm love began freezing and
  froze,
While he took to teasing, and cruelly tose
The girl he had wished to be squeezing and
  squoze.

"Wretch!" he cried, when she threatened to
  leave him, and left,
"How could you deceive me, as you have
  deceft?"
And she answered, "I promised to cleave, and
  I've cleft!"

PLODDING CHANGES.—Some of our plodding readers may like to peruse the following curious variations of the well-known line from Gray's "Elegy," "The ploughman homeward plods his weary way":

The weary ploughman homeward plods his
  way.
The weary ploughman plods his homeward way.

The homeward ploughman plods his weary way.
The homeward ploughman, weary, plods his way.
The homeward, weary, ploughman plods his way.
The weary, homeward ploughman plods his way.
Homeward the weary ploughman plods his way.
Homeward, weary, the ploughman plods his way.
Homeward the ploughman plods his weary way.
Homeward the ploughman, weary, plods his way.
Weary, the homeward ploughman plods his way.
Weary, homeward the ploughman plods his way.
Weary, the ploughman plods his homeward way.

The ploughman plods his homeward, weary way.
The ploughman plods his weary homeward way.
The ploughman homeward, weary, plods his way.
The ploughman, weary, homeward plods his way.
The ploughman, weary, plods his homeward way.

"My Madeline! My Madeline!
　Mark my melodious midnight moans;
　Much may my melting music mean,
　My-modulated monotones.

"My mandolin's mild minstrelsy,
　My mental music magazine,
　My mouth, my mind, my memory,
　Must mingling murmur, 'Madeline.'

"Muster 'mid midnight masquerades,
　Mark Moorish maidens', matrons' mien,

'Mongst Murcia's most majestic maids,
Match me my matchless Madeline.

"Mankind's malevolence may make
Much melancholy music mine;
Many my motives may mistake,
My modest merits much malign.

"My Madeline's most mirthful mood
Much mollifies my mind's machine;
My mournfulness' magnitude
Melts—makes me merry, Madeline!

"Match-making mas may machinate,
Manœuvring misses me misween;
Mere money may make many mate,
My magic motto's—'Madeline!'

"Melt, most mellifluous melody,
'Midst Murcia's misty mounts marine,
Meet me by moonlight—marry me,
Madonna mia!—Madeline."

It is well known that the letter *e* is used more than any other letter in the English alphabet. Each of the following verses contains every letter of the alphabet except the letter *e*:

"A jovial swain should not complain
    Of any buxom fair
Who mocks his pain and thinks it gain
    To quiz his awkward air.

"Quixotic boys who look for joys,
    Quixotic hazards run;
A lass annoys with trivial toys,
    Opposing man for fun.

"A jovial swain may rack his brain,
    And tax his fancy's might;
To quiz is vain, for 'tis most plain
    That what I say is right."

Northampton (England) Courier.

Here is the result of a rhyming punster's efforts:

"A pretty deer is dear to me,
  A hare with downy hair,
A hart I love with all my heart,
  But barely bear a bear.

"'Tis plain that no one takes a plane
  To pare a pair of pears,
Although a rake may take a rake
  To tear away the tares.

"Sol's rays raise thyme, time raises all,
  And through the whole holes wears.
A scribe in writing right may write
  To write and still be wrong;
For write and rite are neither right,
  And don't to right belong.

"Robertson is not Robert's son,
  Nor did he rob Burt's son,
Yet Robert's sun is Robin's sun,
  And everybody's sun.

"Beer often brings a bier to man,
    Coughing a coffin brings,
And too much ale will make us ail,
    As well as other things.

"The person lies who says he lies
    When he is not reclining;
And when consumptive folks decline,
    They all decline declining.

"Quails do not quail before a storm.
    A bow will bow before it;
We cannot rein the rain at all,
    No earthly power reigns o'er it.

"The dyer dyes awhile, then dies—
    To dye he's always trying;
Until upon his dying bed
    He thinks no more of dyeing.

"A son of Mars mars many a son,
    All Deys must have their days;

And every knight should pray each night
    To him who weighs his ways.

"'Tis meet that man should mete out meat
    To feed one's fortune's sun;
The fair should fare on love alone,
    Else one cannot be won.

"Alas, a lass is sometimes false;
    Of faults a maid is made;
Her waist is but a barren waste—
    Though stayed she is not staid.

"The springs shoot forth each spring and shoots
    Shoot forward one and all;
Though summer kills the flowers, it leaves
    The leaves to fall in fall.

"I would a story here commence,
    But you might think it stale;
So we'll suppose that we have reached
    The tail end of our tale."

And here is a zoölogical romance, by C. F. Adams, inspired by an unusual flow of animal spirits:

> No sweeter girl ewe ever gnu
> Than Betty Martin's daughter Sue.
>
> With sable hare, small tapir waist,
> And lips you'd gopher miles to taste;
>
> Bright, lambent eyes, like the gazelle,
> Sheep pertly brought to bear so well;
>
> Ape pretty lass it was avowed,
> Of whom her marmot to be proud.
>
> Deer girl! I loved her as my life,
> And vowed to heifer for my wife.
>
> Alas! A sailor on the sly,
> Had cast on her his wether eye.
>
> He said my love for her was bosh,
> And my affection I musquash.

How she can be oddly wrote. 83

He'd dog her footsteps everywhere,
Anteater in the easy-chair;

He'd setter round, this sailor chap,
And pointer out upon the map

Where once a pirate cruiser boar
Him captive to a foreign shore.

The cruel captain far outdid
The yaks and crimes of Robert Kid.

He oft would whale Jack with the cat,
And say, "My buck, doe you like that?

"What makes you stag around so, say?
The catamounts to something, hey?"

Then he would seal it with an oath,
And say: "You are a lazy sloth!

"I'll starve you down, my sailor fine,
Until for beef and porcupine!"

And, fairly horse with fiendish laughter,
Would say, "Henceforth, mind what giraffe
    ter!"

In short, the many risks he ran
Might well a llama braver man;

Then he was wrecked and castor shore
While feebly clinging to anoa;

Hyena cleft among the rocks
He crept, *sans* shoes and minus ox.

And when he fain would go to bed,
He had to lion leaves instead.

Then Sue would say, with troubled face,
"How koodoo live in such a place?"

And straightway into tears would melt,
And say, "How badger must have felt!"

While he, the brute, woodchuck her chin,
And say, "Aye-aye, my lass!" and grin.

* * * * * *

Excuse these steers. . . . It's over now;
There's naught like grief the hart can cow.

Jackass'd her to be his, and she—
She gave Jackal, and jilted me.

And now, alas! the little minks
Is bound to him with Hymen's lynx.
—*Detroit Free Press.*

While upon the subject of puns, we might quote the following, clipped from the "Graphic":

"On being consulted about it Spikes says that Uncle Sam aunticipates the transfer of the Indian Bureau to some mother department, and if this should father improve the condition of the children of the forest, in sondry ways, by cousin them to be more comfortable, it would be a niece arrangement and daughter be made." We are inclined, in nephew instances, to agree with the gramma, but not the spelling.

The "Graphic" is also responsible for the following English stanza transformed into Russian, said to have been found in a room after it had been vacated by Alexis while in this country. It is introduced as an example of how "she can be oddly wrote":

> "Owata jollitimiv ad
> Sinci tooklevov mioldad!
> Owata merricoviv bin—
> Ivespenta nawful pilovtin!
> Damsorri tolevami now,
> But landigoshenjingo vow,
> Thetur kishwar mustavastop
> Gotele graphitoff topop."

The following clever paraphrase of the old rhythmic story of "Jack's House" is a good illustration of the scope and flexibility of our language, and suggests the fact that tautological errors of writing need seldom be committed.

Behold the mansion reared by dædal Jack.

See the malt stored in many a plethoric sack,
In the proud cirque of Ivan's bivouac.

Mark how the Rat's felonious fangs invade
The golden stores in John's pavilion laid.

Anon, with velvet foot and Tarquin strides,
Subtle Grimalkin to his quarry glides—
Grimalkin grim, that slew the fierce *rodent*
Whose tooth insidious Johann's sackcloth rent.

Lo! now the deep-mouthed canine foe's assault,
That vexed the avenger of the stolen malt,
Stored in the hallowed precincts of that hall
That rose complete at Jack's creative call.

Here stalks the impetuous Cow with crumpled
    horn,
Whereon the exacerbating hound was torn,
Who bayed the feline slaughter-beast that slew
The Rat predaceous, whose keen fangs ran
    through
The textile fibers that involved the grain
That lay in Hans' inviolate domain.

Here walks forlorn the Damsel, crowned with
    rue,
Lactiferous spoils from vaccine dugs, who drew
Of that corniculate beast whose tortuous horn
Tossed to the clouds, in fierce vindictive scorn,
The harrowing hound, whose braggart bark
    and stir
Arched the lithe spine and reared the indig-
    nant fur
Of Puss, that with verminicidal claw
Struck the weird Rat, in whose insatiate maw
Lay reeking malt, that erst in Ivan's courts we saw

Robed in senescent garb that seems in sooth
Too long a prey to Chronos' iron tooth.

Behold the man whose amorous lips incline,
Full with young Eros' osculative sign,
To the lorn maiden whose lact-albic hands,
Drew albu-lactic wealth from lacteal glands
Of that immortal bovine, by whose horn
Distort, to realm ethereal was borne
The beast catulean, vexer of that sly
Ulysses quadrupedal, who made die
The old mordacious Rat, that dared devour
Antecedaneous Ale, in John's domestic bower.

Lo, here, with hirsute honors doffed, succinct
Of saponaceous locks, the Priest who linked
In Hymen's golden bands the torn unthrift,
Whose means exiguous stared from many a rift,
Even as he kissed the virgin all forlorn,
Who milked the cow with implicated horn,

Who in fine wrath the canine torturer skied,
That dared to vex the insidious muricide,
Who let the auroral effluence through the pelt
Of the sly Rat that robbed the palace Jack had
      built.

The loud cantankerous Shanghai comes at last,
Whose shouts arouse the shorn ecclesiast,
Who sealed the vows of Hymen's sacrament,
To him who robed in garments indigent,
Exosculates the damsel lachrymose,
The emulgator of that horned brute morose,
That tossed the dog, that worried the cat, that *kilt*
The Rat that ate the malt, that lay in the house
      that Jack built.

VII.

By the Untutored.

CARE should be taken in writing for the young, or they may get a wholly different meaning from the language than that intended. The Bishop of Hereford was examining a school-class one day, and, among other things, asked what an average was. Several boys pleaded ignorance, but one at last replied, "It is what a hen lays on." This answer puzzled the bishop not a little; but the boy persisted in it, stating that he had read it in his little book of facts. He was then told to bring the little book, and, on doing so, he pointed triumphantly to a paragraph commencing, "The domestic hen lays *on an average* fifty eggs each year."

If English is "wrote" as she is often "spoke" by the ignorant and careless, she would bear little resemblance to the original Queen's English. A listener wrote out a short conversation heard the other day between two pupils of a high-school, and here is the phonetic result:

"Warejergo lasnight?"
"Hadder skate."
"Jerfind th'ice hard'n'good?"
"Yes, hard'nough."
"Jer goerlone?"
"No; Bill'n Joe wenterlong."
"Howlate jerstay?"
"Pastate."
"Lemmeknow wenyergoagin, woncher? I wantergo'n'show yer howterskate."

"H'm, ficoodn't skate better'n you I'd sell-out'n'quit."

"Well, we'll tryeranc'n'seefyercan."

Here, as they took different streets, their conversation ceased.

A writer in the "School-boy Magazine" has gathered together the following dictionary words as defined by certain small people:

Bed-time—Shut eye time.
Dust—Mud with the juice squeezed out.
Fan—A thing to brush warm off with.
Fins—A fish's wings.
Ice—Water that staid out in the cold and went to sleep.
Monkey—A very small boy with a tail.
Nest-Egg—The egg that the old hen measures by, to make new ones.
Pig—A hog's little boy.
Salt—What makes your potato taste bad when you don't put any on.

Snoring—Letting off sleep.

Stars—The moon's eggs.

Wakefulness—Eyes all the time coming unbuttoned.

The following specimens from scholars' examinations in making sentences to illustrate the definitions of words, found in their small dictionaries, will have a familiar sound to some of our readers:

Frantic = Wild: I picked a bouquet of frantic flowers.

Retorted = Returned: We retorted home at six o'clock.

Summoned = Called: I summoned to see Mary last week.

Athletic = Strong: The vinegar was too athletic to be used.

Poignant = Sharp: My knife is very poignant.

Ordinances = Rules: We learned the ordinances for finding the greatest common divisor.

Turbid = Muddy : The road was so turbid that we stuck fast in the mud.

Tandem = One behind another : The scholars sit tandem in school.

Akimbo = With a crook : I saw a dog with an akimbo in his tail.

Atonement = Satisfaction : There is no atonement in boat-riding in a cold day.

Composure = Calmness : The composure of the day was remarkable.

We have the authority of the late Dr. Hart as to the genuineness of the following extracts, taken from the papers of a class seeking admission into a high-school, to which had been given a list of words for their meanings and applications :

Fabulous—Full of threads : Silk is fabulous.

Accession—The act of eating a great deal :

John got very sick after dinner by accession.

Atonement—A small insect: Queen Mab was pulled by atonements.

Develop—To swallow up: God sent a whale to develop Jonah.

Circumference—Distance through the middle: Distance around the middle of the outside.

Mobility—Belonging to the people: The mobility of St. Louis has greatly increased.

Adequate—A land animal: An elephant is an adequate.

Gregarious—Pertaining to idols: The Sandwich-Islanders are gregarious.

Fluctuation—Coming in great numbers: There was a great fluctuation of immigrants.

Alternate—Not ternate.

Intrinsic—Not trinsic; weak, feeble: He was a very intrinsic old man.

Subservient—One opposed to the upholding of servants.

Don't:
A Manual of Mistakes and Improprieties more or less prevalent in Conduct and Speech.

"I'll view the manners of the town."—*Comedy of Errors.*

By CENSOR.

Square 16mo.   Parchment paper.   Price, 30 cents.

English as She is Spoke;
or, A Jest in Sober Earnest.

Compiled from the celebrated "NEW GUIDE OF CONVERSATION IN PORTUGUESE AND ENGLISH."

"Excruciatingly funny."—*London World.*

"Every one who loves a laugh should either buy, beg, borrow, or—we had almost said steal—the book."—*London Fun.*

Square 16mo.   Parchment-paper cover.   Price, 30 cents.

New York: D. APPLETON & CO., 1, 3, & 5 Bond Street.

Write and Speak Correctly.

The Orthoëpist:

A Pronouncing Manual, containing about Three Thousand Five Hundred Words, including a considerable Number of the Names of Foreign Authors, Artists, etc., that are often mispronounced. By ALFRED AYRES. Fourteenth edition. 18mo, cloth, extra. Price, $1.00.

"It gives us pleasure to say that we think the author in the treatment of this very difficult and intricate subject, English pronunciation, gives proof of not only an unusual degree of orthoëpical knowledge, but also, for the most part, of rare judgment and taste."—JOSEPH THOMAS, LL. D., *in Literary World.*

The Verbalist:

A Manual devoted to Brief Discussions of the Right and the Wrong Use of Words, and to some other Matters of Interest to those who would Speak and Write with Propriety, including a Treatise on Punctuation. By ALFRED AYRES, author of "The Orthoëpist." Ninth edition. 18mo, cloth, extra. Price, $1.00.

"We remain shackled by timidity till we have learned to speak with propriety."—JOHNSON.

New York: D. APPLETON & CO., 1, 3, & 5 Bond Street.

Social Etiquette of New York.

CONTENTS:

The Value of Etiquette; Introductions; Solicitations; Strangers in Towns; Débuts in Society; Visiting, and Visiting Cards for Ladies; Card and Visiting Customs for Gentlemen; Morning Receptions and Kettle-Drums; Giving and attending Parties, Balls, and Germans; Dinner-giving and Dining out; Breakfasts, Luncheons, and Suppers; Opera and Theatre Parties, Private Theatricals, and Musicales; Extended Visits; Customs and Costumes at Theatres, Concerts, and Operas (being two additional chapters written for this edition); Etiquette of Weddings (rewritten, for this edition, in accordance with the latest fashionable usage); Christenings and Birthdays; Marriage Anniversaries; New Year's Day in New York; Funeral Customs and Seasons of Mourning.

18mo, cloth, gilt, price, $1.00.

New York: D. APPLETON & CO., 1, 3, & 5 Bond Street.

Errors in the Use of English.

By the late WILLIAM B. HODGSON, LL. D.,

Professor of Political Economy in the University of Edinburgh. American revised edition. 12mo, cloth. Price, $1.50.

"The most comprehensive and useful of the many books designed to promote correctness in English composition by furnishing examples of inaccuracy, is the volume compiled by the late William B. Hodgson, under the title of 'Errors in the Use of English.' The American edition of this treatise, now published by the Appletons, has been revised, and in many respects materially improved, by Francis A. Teall, who seldom differs from the author without advancing satisfactory reasons for his opinion. The capital merits of this work are that it is founded on actual blunders, verified by chapter and verse reference, and that the breaches of good use to which exception is taken have been committed, not by slipshod, uneducated writers, of whom nothing better could be expected, but by persons distinguished for more than ordinary carefulness in respect to style."—*New York Sun*.

New York: D. APPLETON & CO., 1, 3, & 5 Bond Street.

"'Bachelor Bluff' is bright, witty, keen, deep, sober, philosophical, amusing, instructive, philanthropic—in short, what is not 'Bachelor Bluff'?"

NEW CHEAP SUMMER EDITION, IN PARCHMENT PAPER.

Bachelor Bluff:

His Opinions, Sentiments, and Disputations. By OLIVER B. BUNCE.

"Mr. Bunce is a writer of uncommon freshness and power. . . . Those who have read his brief but carefully written studies will value at their true worth the genuine critical insight and fine literary qualities which characterize his work."—*Christian Union.*

"We do not recall any volume of popular essays published of late years which contains so much good writing, and so many fine and original comments on topics of current interest. Mr. Oracle Bluff is a self-opinionated, genial, whole-souled fellow. . . . His talk is terse, epigrammatic, full of quotable proverbs and isolated bits of wisdom."—*Boston Traveller.*

"It is a book which, while professedly aiming to amuse, and affording a very rare and delightful fund of amusement, insinuates into the crevices of the reflective mind thoughts and sentiments that are sure to fructify and perpetuate themselves."—*Eclectic Magazine.*

New cheap edition. 16mo, parchment paper. Price, 50 cents.

New York: D. APPLETON & CO., 1, 3, & 5 Bond Street.

Hygiene for Girls.

By Irenæus P. Davis, M. D.

18mo, cloth.   Price, $1.25.

"Many a woman whose childhood was bright with promise endures an after-life of misery because, through a false delicacy, she remained ignorant of her physical nature and requirements, although on all other subjects she may be well-informed; and so at length she goes to her grave mourning the hard fate that has made existence a burden, and perhaps wondering to what end she was born, when a little knowledge at the proper time would have shown her how to easily avoid those evils that have made her life a wretched failure."—*From Introduction*.

"A very useful book for parents who have daughters is 'Hygiene for Girls,' by Irenæus P. Davis, M. D., published by D. Appleton & Co. And it is just the book for an intelligent, well-instructed girl to read with care. It is not a text-book, nor does it bristle with technical terms. But it tells in simple language just what girls should do and not to do to preserve the health and strength, to realize the joys, and prepare for the duties of a woman's lot. It is written with a delicacy, too, which a mother could hardly surpass in talking with her daughter."—*Christian at Work*.

New York: D. APPLETON & CO., 1, 3, & 5 Bond Street.

PRICE, $1.25 A VOL.]   [IN TWELVE VOLS.

THE

Parchment Shakspere.

NEW EDITION OF SHAKSPERE'S WORKS,

Bound in parchment, uncut, gilt top.

New York:
D. APPLETON AND COMPANY,
1, 3, AND 5 BOND STREET.

This edition is being printed with new type, cast expressly for the work, on laid linen paper, and in a form and style which give it peculiar elegance. The text is mainly that of DELIUS, the chief difference consisting in a more sparing use of punctuation than that employed by the well-known German editor. Wherever a variant reading is adopted, some good and recognized SHAKSPEREAN critic has been followed. In no case is a new rendering of the text proposed; nor has it been thought necessary to distract the reader's attention by notes or comments.

"*There is, perhaps, no edition in which the works of Shakspere can be read in such luxury of type, and quiet distinction of form, as this.*"—PALL MALL GAZETTE.

The English Grammar
of William Cobbett.

Carefully revised and annotated by
ALFRED AYRES,
Author of "The Orthoëpist," "The Verbalist," etc.

"The only amusing grammar in the world."—HENRY LYTTON BULWER.

"Interesting as a story-book."—HAZLITT.

"I know it well, and have read it with great admiration."—RICHARD GRANT WHITE.

"Cobbett's Grammar is probably the most readable grammar ever written. For the purposes of self-education it is unrivaled."—*From the Preface.*

Mr. Ayres makes a feature of the fact that WHO and WHICH *are properly the* CO-ORDINATING *relative pronouns*, and that THAT *is properly the* RESTRICTIVE *relative pronoun.*

The Grammar has an Index covering no less than eight pages.

Uniform with "The Orthoëpist" and "The Verbalist."
18mo, cloth. Price, $1.00.

New York: D. APPLETON & CO., 1, 3, & 5 Bond Street.

This book is a preservation photocopy
produced on Weyerhaeuser acid free
Cougar Opaque 50# book weight paper,
which meets the requirements of
ANSI/NISO Z39.48-1992 (permanence of paper)

Preservation photocopying and binding
by
Acme Bookbinding
Charlestown, Massachusetts

1994